CHINA

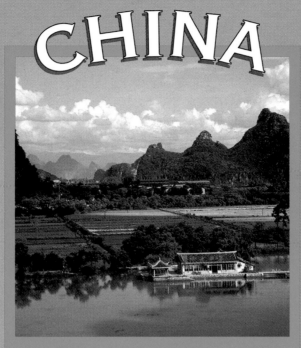

A TRUE BOOK

by
Ann Heinrichs

Children's Press®

A Division of Grolier Publishing

New York London Hong Kong Sydney
Danbury, Connecticut

Reading Consultant
Linda Cornwell
Learning Resource Consultant
Indiana Department of
Education

Dedicated to the memory
of Dick Gway Yee
(1914-1993),
a wise and gentle man

A Chinese child

Library of Congress Cataloging-in-Publication Data

Heinrichs, Ann.
    China / by Ann Heinrichs.
        p.   cm. — (A true book)
    Age 7-9, 2-4.
    Includes index.
    Summary: Introduces the history, geography, economy, people,
and culture of the country with the largest population in the world.
    ISBN 0-516-20329-0 (lib.bdg.)   0-516-26165-7 (pbk.)
    1. China—Juvenile literature. [1. China.] I. Title. II. Series.
DS706.H395   1997
951—dc20   96-24972
                                                                    CIP
                                                                    AC

Contents

The Land   5

The People   9

The Early Dynasties   14

From Dynasty to Republic   18

How People Live   25

Farms and Factories   34

Culture and Arts   38

To Find Out More   44

Important Words   46

Index   47

Meet the Author   48

The Land

China is a vast country in eastern Asia. It is the third-largest country in the world, after Russia and Canada. China borders the Pacific Ocean. Most of China's largest cities are along the east coast, where the land is low and flat. Rice paddies—

water-covered fields—cover these lowlands. Farther inland, snow-capped mountains tower over the landscape. China's highest region is the Tibetan Plateau in the southwest. The huge Gobi and Taklimakan deserts stretch across the north. China's major rivers are the Yangtze and the Hwang He, which is also called the Yellow River. Both flow eastward into the sea.

Rice grows in water-covered fields called paddies (above). Northern China consists of huge desert regions (left).

China's rivers have always played an important role in trade and travel.

Horses, camels, and foxes live in northern China. Giant pandas and different kinds of monkeys are found in China's southern region.

The People

More than one billion people live in China. That means about one of every five people on Earth is Chinese.

There are many dialects, or forms, of the Chinese language. Mandarin is China's official dialect. It is used in schools and businesses. The Chinese write with

A crowded street in China (left);
Chinese character writing (above)

characters, or symbols, instead
of letters. Each character stands
for a complete word or an idea.
There are more than forty
thousand Chinese characters.

China's largest cities include
Beijing (the nation's capital),

Shanghai, Tianjin, and Guangzhou. Because the cities are so crowded, the government controls the number of people who may live there.

The city of Beijing is the capital of China.

Speaking Chinese

Chinese is a very difficult language to speak. On the next page are examples of letter sounds in Chinese words. **Use the key to pronounce them** the way the Chinese do!

OPEN

歡迎光臨

LYNCH SIGN CO. LONG BEACH, CA. 81-CH

Letters	Say...	Example	Say...
ao	"ow" as in "now"	hao	how
q	"ch" as in "chin"	Qin	chin
x	"sh" as in "she"	xin	shin
z	"ds" as in "kids"	zi	dzee
zh	"j" as in "jump"	Zhou	Joe

The Early Dynasties

For thousands of years, China was ruled by dynasties, or powerful families. Members of the same family ruled until another family started a new dynasty.

China's earliest dynasties began almost four thousand years ago. During the Qin dynasty (221 B.C.–206 B.C.), the

emperor wanted to protect China from invaders. He ordered construction of the Great Wall across northern China. The Great Wall is still standing. It is about 1,500 miles (2,413 kilometers) long.

In the A.D.1200s, fierce warriors called Mongols invaded China. Their leader, Kublai Khan, began the Yuan dynasty. Kublai Khan ruled from the city that is now Beijing.

In 1275, a young man named Marco Polo arrived at Kublai Khan's court. Marco had traveled to China from his home in Italy. He stayed in China for the next seventeen years. When he returned to

Kublai Khan (left) is the best-known Mongol warrior in China's history. Marco Polo (right) is famous for the seventeen years he spent in the court of Kublai Khan.

Italy, Marco Polo's reports sparked great interest in China among Europeans.

From Dynasty to Republic

A leader named Hongwu led a revolt against the Mongols in 1368. Hongwu's son, Emperor Yongle, built a royal city in Beijing. It was called the Forbidden City. The Forbidden City had many palaces and other beautiful buildings. Common citizens were not allowed inside.

A modern view of the Forbidden City, which was used only by the emperor and his court.

During the Ming dynasty, ships from Europe began sailing to China. About 1600, Roman Catholic missionaries arrived from Portugal.

Next, Manchu warriors from the northeast invaded China. They set up the Qing dynasty (1644-1912).

A two-year-old boy named Pu Yi became the last emperor of China in 1908. He reigned until 1912, when a revolt led by Sun Yat-sen threw out the Manchus. China then became a republic that was headed by a president. The days of the dynasties had come to an end.

Manchu warriors (above) invaded China in 1644 and established the Qing dynasty. Sun Yat-sen (left) led a revolt against the Manchus in 1912.

The republic was over-thrown by communists in 1949. They were led by Mao Zedong.

The leader of China at the time of the revolt was Chiang Kai-shek. He and his followers fled to the island of Taiwan.

Mao Zedong made China a communist country and gave it a new name—the People's Republic of China. When emperors ruled China, the royal families were very rich.

Mao Zedong renamed China the People's Republic of China.

But average Chinese citizens were very poor. When Mao took control of China, he made changes so that everyone would be equal: nobody would be rich and nobody would be poor. But Mao also destroyed many beloved Chinese traditions. Mao ruled China until he died in 1976. Some leaders have tried to make China more democratic, but it is still a communist country.

How People Live

While Mao was alive, most Chinese people dressed alike. Both men and women wore simple, loose-fitting shirts and pants. The peoples' clothing was usually dark colored.

After Mao died, however, clothing styles changed. In the cities, women began

This man doing morning exercises is dressed in the style of clothing ordered by Mao Zedong.

wearing colorful dresses. Men began to wear suits, sport coats, and ties. Jeans and T-shirts became popular. But in the countryside, many people still dress in the old communist style.

Most city people live in tall apartment buildings made of brick or concrete. Inside, each apartment is very small—only two or three rooms. Most city dwellings have electric lights.

China's cities are very crowded, and most people live in small apartments.

Kitchens have running water. But few homes have their own showers and toilets. These are located in central areas where many people can use them.

Houses in small villages are made of stone, mud bricks, or concrete blocks. Most of the houses are larger than city apartments. Oil lamps provide light. People burn wood or straw for cooking and heating.

Houses in a rural Chinese village

Rice is the main ingredient in most Chinese meals. Chopsticks are more common than forks and knives.

The Chinese eat fresh foods that are low in fat. In some areas, rice is eaten at every meal. Grains such as wheat and millet are made into noodles or dumplings. Other popular foods are cabbage, squash, leafy green vegetables, peaches, and bananas.

Most people in China eat using chopsticks instead of knives and forks. Children begin using chopsticks when they are very young and soon become experts.

Giant Pandas

The only place in the world where giant pandas are found in the wild is in southern China. Giant pandas are peaceful, shy animals that spend most of their time in the forest eating bamboo.

When a giant panda is born, it is very tiny. It weighs only 5 ounces (140 grams)! Adult pandas are 3.5 to 5 feet (1.2 to 1.5 meters) long and weigh up to 350 pounds (160 kilograms).

Farms and Factories

Three of every five Chinese people work on farms. In 1958, the communist government made all the farms into communes. Each commune was made up of several hundred families. All of the families owned and worked the land together.

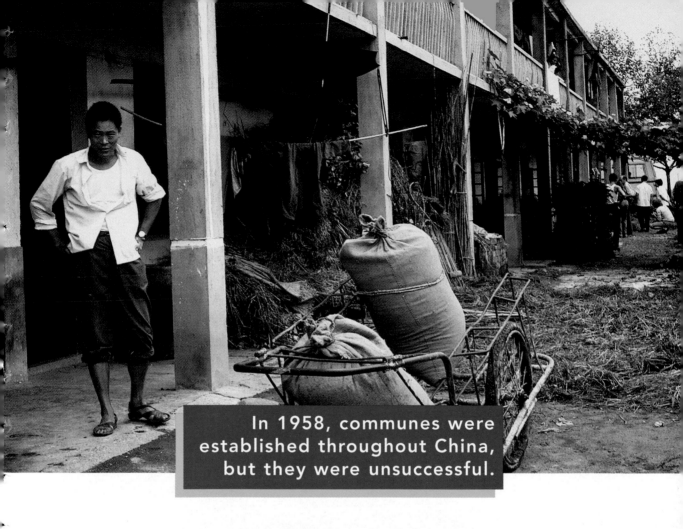

In 1958, communes were established throughout China, but they were unsuccessful.

In 1979, the farming system changed again. Families were put in charge of their own farms.

Today, major farm crops are rice, wheat, cotton, fruits, and vegetables. Some farmers also raise chickens and pigs.

The women in this factory are assembling electric appliances.

Many Chinese work in factories or in the shipping business. Gigantic ships sail into China's seaports from all over the world. They bring machines, cloth, iron, chemicals, and grains. Some of these products go to China's factories. There, workers make clothing, shoes, toys, telephones, radios, and many other goods. These goods are then exported, or shipped to other countries.

Culture and Arts

The Chinese calendar follows the cycles of the moon. Chinese New Year usually comes with February's full moon. People celebrate with fireworks and colorful dragon dances in the streets.

An animal is matched with each year. For example, 1997 is

Dragon dances mark the Chinese New Year.

the Year of the Ox, 1998 is the
Year of the Tiger, 1999 is the
Year of the Hare (Rabbit), and
2000 is the Year of the Dragon.
During their long history,
the Chinese developed many

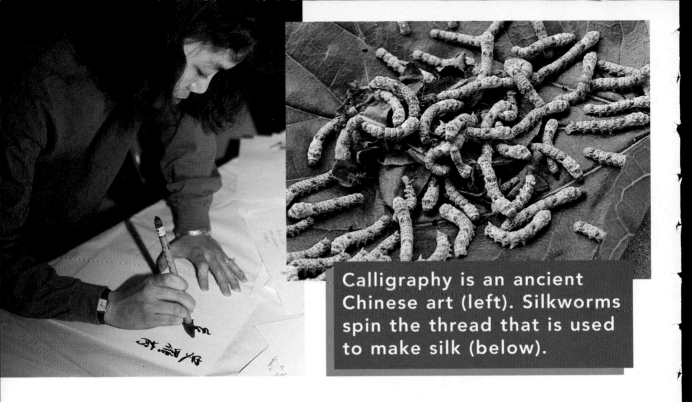

Calligraphy is an ancient Chinese art (left). Silkworms spin the thread that is used to make silk (below).

fine arts and crafts. The Chinese are noted for their beautiful calligraphy—hand-writing with a brush and ink.

The Chinese began making silk almost four thousand years ago. Silkworms spun the shiny threads, which the Chinese wove into delicate and beautiful cloth.

One of China's greatest teachers was Confucius, who lived during the 500s B.C. He taught that all people should respect each other. Many

Confucius was a great philosopher whose teachings were honored in China for hundreds of years.

Chinese still follow the teachings of Confucius.

Buddhism came to China from India. Buddha, its founder, taught unselfishness and kindness to others. The Chinese built temples where they could honor Buddha.

Many Buddhist temples can be found in China.

Chinese children hope for a bright future.

These and other teachings are rejected by China's government. But their many ancient traditions have helped to make the Chinese people who they are today.

43

To Find Out More

Here are some additional resources to help you learn more about the nation of China:

 **Books**

 **Organizations**

Charley, Catherine. **China.** Raintree Steck-Vaughn, 1995.

Mac Millan, Dianne M. **Chinese New Year.** Enslow, 1994.

Steele, Philip. **The Giant Panda.** Kingfisher, 1994.

Zurlo, Tony. **China: The Dragon Awakes.** Dillon, 1994.

Embassy of the People's Republic of China
2300 Connecticut Ave., NW
Washington, DC 20008

World Wildlife Fund (WWF)
1250 24th Street, NW
Washington, DC 20037

United Nations Information Centre
1775 K Street, NW
Washington, DC 20008

Online Sites

China Tour
http://www.ihep.ac.cn/tour/china_tour.html

Visit the provinces of mainland China; see maps, photos, and more.

Friends of China
http://beloit.edu/~milleres/

Get your "fortune cookie of the day," learn to speak Chinese, receive the latest news from the world of Ping-Pong, or check out the weather in Beijing.

The Panda Room
http://www.xroads.com/~pct/panda.html

Provides information about pandas, as well as pictures and links to other sites

Planet Earth Home Page — China
http://corpinex.nosc.mil/planet_earth/countries/China.html

Includes facts about China, as well as different cities and regions; virtual tours and related sites are also available

Window on China
http://www.eecs.ukans.edu/

~btwang/China/China.html

Here you'll find facts about China, news, entertainment, art, history, and even a virtual Chinatown!

Important Words

communist form of government in which the leaders control a country's citizens

concrete hard material for making sidewalks and buildings

millet grass with small grain that is used for food

missionaries people sent to a foreign country to teach religion to its inhabitants

republic form of government that is led by a president, instead of a king or queen

revolt uprising against the government

traditions long-held beliefs and customs

Index

(**Boldface** page numbers
indicate illustrations.)

Beijing, 10–11, **11**, 16,
    18
Buddha, 42
Buddhism, 42
calligraphy, 40, **40**
Chiang Kai-shek, 22
Chinese New Year, 38–39
chopsticks, **30**, 31
communes, 34, **35**
communist, 22, 24, 26,
    34
Confucius, 41–42, **41**
dragon dances, 38, **39**
dynasties, 14–15, 20
Emperor Yongle, 18
factories, 37
Forbidden City, 18, **19**
giant pandas, 8
Gobi Desert, 6
Great Wall, 15, **15**
Guangzhou, 11

Hongwu, 18
Hwang He River, 6
Kublai Khan, 16, **17**
Manchu warriors, 20, **21**
Mandarin, 9
Mao Zedong, 22–24, **23,**
    25
Marco Polo, 16–17, **17**
Ming dynasty, 19
Mongols, 16, 18
Pu Yi, 20
Qin dynasty, 14–15
Qing dynasty, 20
republic, 20, 22
rice paddies, 5–6, **7**
Shanghai, 11
silkworms, 40–41, **40**
Sun Yat-sen, 20, **21**
Taklimakan Desert, 6
Tianjin, 11
Tibetan Plateau, 6
Yangtze River, 6
Yellow River. *See* Hwang
    He River

Meet the Author

Ann Heinrichs grew up in Arkansas and lives in Chicago, Illinois. She has written more than twenty books about American, Asian, and African history and culture. She has also written numerous newspaper, magazine, and encyclopedia articles.

Besides the United States, she has traveled in Europe, North Africa, the Middle East, and east Asia. The desert is her favorite terrain.

Ms. Heinrichs holds bachelor's and master's degrees in piano performance. For relaxation, she practices chi gung and t'ai chi.

L